POCAHONTAS
Coloring Book

BRIAN DOHERTY

Illustrated by Thea Kliros

DOVER PUBLICATIONS, INC.
New York

Bibliographical Note

Pocahontas Coloring Book is a new work, first published by Dover Publications, Inc., in 1994.

DOVER *Pictorial Archive* SERIES

International Standard Book Number: 0-486-28040-3

Manufactured in the United States of America
Dover Publications, Inc., 31 East 2nd Street, Mineola, N.Y. 11501

IN THE WINTER OF 1606, three English ships, the *Susan Constant*, the *Godspeed* and the *Discovery*, started across the Atlantic under the command of Captain Christopher Newport. They carried 105 men, intending to settle at Roanoke Island, where an English colony had disappeared twenty years before, but they were driven further north by a storm. After many months at sea, they began hunting for a suitable place for settlement. They sailed into the broad opening of Chesapeake Bay and were still moving northward when they encountered a wide river that flowed into the bay from the mainland on the west. They turned their ships into this river, which they called the James, in honor of their king, and studied the shores for an inviting spot to land.

There were men and women in this land, descendants of those who had lived there for unknown ages. They were standing on the shore, watching the approaching vessels. When the *Susan Constant*, which was a hundred yards ahead of the smaller boats, pulled up alongside this group, two of the warriors on the bank let their arrows fly.

Captain Newport suggested they fire their guns into the party.

"No, we should cultivate their good will. We will need their friendship, and must not use our guns as long as our lives can be saved without them."

This remark was made by a man standing at the prow, spyglass in hand. He was of sturdy build, in well-to-do civilian's clothing, with a full beard and a huge mustache. His resolute face was deeply tanned. He was not yet thirty years of age and appeared stronger than the officers and crew around him. He was Captain John Smith, whose services would later earn him the name, "Father of Virginia."

By the afternoon of the next day, the three vessels had traveled eighty miles from the river's mouth and were now approaching the peninsula where they had decided to make camp. Suddenly everyone's attention was turned upstream. Captain Smith lifted his telescope to his eyes. Around a bend in the river a canoe shot into sight. Captain Newport, who also had a glass, stood near Smith and studied the small craft as well.

"Those two warriors have more courage than their friends," Newport remarked.

"There is only one warrior in the canoe," replied Smith, gazing through his telescope; "the other is a girl."

Seated in the middle of the canoe was an Indian youth who was less than twenty years old. Propelling the boat, he faced the vessels downriver. He had long, black hair about his shoulders, and his face was stained with the juice of the *puccoon*, or bloodroot. His chest was bare but his waist was clasped with a deerskin girdle, with leggings that reached to his beaded moccasins. He was a fine warrior despite his youth.

The other occupant of the little craft was the youth's sister. She was no more than twelve years old, with beautiful features. She had thrown back her doeskin robe, lined with wood dove's down. She wore coral bracelets on her wrists and ankles, and a white plume in her abundant hair.

Her leggings and skirt were similar to her brother's, but she wore a doeskin jacket that covered her arms to the elbow. Her face was not treated with the red juice that her brother used. This girl could speed through the woods like a deer, shoot an arrow with the accuracy of a veteran warrior, swim like a fish and read nature's signs the way we might read a book.

Nantaquas, as the young man was called, and his sister, Pocahontas, had left their home a long way up the river, paddling downstream, when, rounding a bend in the river, they were startled by the sight of the three ships slowly coming up the river with white sails spread. Nantaquas stopped for a moment while both gazed at the sight. When Pocahontas had looked for several minutes in amazement at the European ships, watching the men on the decks, she asked:

"Why are they coming to the country of Powhatan?"

"I don't know," her brother replied, "maybe they intend to take away our hunting grounds."

"How can that be," the girl laughed, "when the warriors of Powhatan are like the leaves on the trees? There are only a handful of the white folk—we have nothing to fear from them. Let's visit the big canoes."

The youth increased the speed of his boat, drawing rapidly near the *Susan Constant*, whose passengers and crew watched his approach with curiosity. Nantaquas doubted the wisdom of his sister's wishes. She believed that any people who were treated kindly would return the same treatment. But Nantaquas recalled stories of the white men that were not to their credit. Some of them had slain Indians as though they were animals; they had treated them with great cruelty and repaid kindness with brutality. Nantaquas also remembered that there had been an English settlement at Roanoke Island, but that was before he was born. Whether those settlers had been killed by the Indians, or whether they had joined the friendly tribes who perhaps rescued them from starvation, Nantaquas did not know. He was sure, though, that he and his sister must be very careful.

Captain Smith called out, "Welcome! Welcome! Won't you come aboard that we may shake hands and break bread with you?"

Although Nantaquas and his sister did not understand the words, the gestures of the men were clear.

"Why do you hesitate?" Pocahontas asked impatiently. "They want to greet us—don't be ungrateful."

But Nantaquas was decisive: "They are strangers—we have heard evil things of many of them. We shall go no closer."

In answer to the Englishmen's invitations, Nantaquas raised one hand and waved it toward the ship. He meant it as a polite refusal. Then he sent the canoe skimming upstream.

Smith noticed a strange thing at this point. He saw a column of smoke filtering upward from among the trees on a wooded elevation inland. It had a wavy motion from side to side. There could be no question that it was a signal fire.

Nantaquas paddled like one who could never tire. His sister was unhappy because he had refused to take her aboard the big canoe. He understood her feeling, and wisely gave her time to get over it. Nevertheless, she was planning her revenge.

The canoe had not yet touched the land when the girl leaped out as lightly as a fawn, not pausing to pick up her bow. Turning around, she grasped the front of the craft, as if to draw it onto the bank. Nantaquas rose to his feet, bending to pick up the bows and arrows. While he was doing so, the girl gave a fast sideways jerk to the boat. Thrown off balance, Nantaquas went backward over the side of the canoe and, as his heels kicked in the air, he dropped out of sight under the water.

Pocahontas screamed with delight. She had punished her brother as she planned. But her brother soon recovered and gave chase. She ran as fast as she could to get away, but ten to fifteen yards ahead stood an Indian, six feet tall, motionless and surveying the couple with an inquiring expression. His long locks were sprinkled with gray, and his face was stern and lined with the passage of many stormy years. He was dressed like the younger warrior except that his face was unstained. In the belt around his waist were thrust a long knife and the handle of a tomahawk, but he carried no bow or quiver.

Hardly had the girl caught sight of him, when she ran forward and, throwing both arms around him, called out in panic: "Father, save me from Nantaquas! He wants to kill me!"

The father gazed at the young man and demanded: "What is the meaning of this?"

This was the famous chieftain, Powhatan. He ruled over numerous tribes, nearly all of whom he had conquered and brought under his sway. From Virginia to the far south he had no equal. Pocahontas, pretty and bright, was his favorite child and she could do no wrong in his eyes. Nantaquas was also a favorite, though he had other worthy sons.

"Let my child go home. Powhatan has something he would say to Nantaquas."

Pocahontas darted from sight and the chieftain continued: "The white men have come across the Deep Water to the hunting grounds of Powhatan and his people."

"Yes," the youth responded, "we met them on the river in their big canoes. They spoke words we did not understand, nor could they understand us. They have come to make their homes among us."

So Powhatan, from this and the signal fires he had read, knew of the coming of the Europeans while they were sailing up the James River, several days before he saw them. Powhatan was deeply disturbed by the arrival of the English.

"They will come to land and build their wigwams. By and by others will come and make their homes beside them; and they will keep on coming, until they are as plentiful as the leaves on the trees. We have heard from the Indians of the south that they bring weapons that shoot fire and slay men who are beyond the reach of our arrows. They will kill our people or drive us into the sea."

"The words of Powhatan are wise," said Nantaquas respectfully. "I am afraid of them and would not trust Pocahontas in their power."

"My son did right. She is but a child; she must stay away from them."

"And what shall be done with the white men?" asked Nantaquas. "Shall they be left alone when they go ashore, that their numbers may increase?"

"When the serpent is small, a child may crush it, but, if left to grow, it will soon sting her to death."

Powhatan held a long meeting with his chiefs and warriors. Plans for the destruction of the colony were drawn up; but before he slept that night, Pocahontas made Powhatan tell her all that had been agreed upon—and she did not rest until he had given his promise to postpone the dreadful work. He would not promise to do more than postpone his designs, but this delay was of the greatest importance to the welfare of the little colony.

The low peninsula that the newcomers had landed on was not an ideal site for a settlement. But the weary travelers decided to take their chances. Anchor was dropped and boats began taking the men and their belongings to shore and there, on May 13, 1607, was founded Jamestown—the first lasting English settlement in the New World.

Soon the settlers were busy building their community. For a while, things went well, but it became clear that many of the men were unfit for the work involved. Many were greedy and lazy, including some of the colony's leaders. Captain Smith, the ablest of them, could not take command because on the voyage across the Atlantic, some of the leaders accused him of trying to take charge of everything. Still waiting to defend himself at a trial, Smith was shut out of the Council. But he did not sulk. "By and by they will ask for me," he thought. He impressed upon his friends the need to keep on good terms with the Indians. The food brought over the ocean would not last more than two or three months, and then it would be necessary to obtain supplies from the Indians.

Distrustful of Powhatan's attitude toward them, Captain Smith and a party of men took the first chance to sail up the river and pay a formal visit to the emperor of the country. The name of Powhatan's capital was also Powhatan, the chieftain being named after the town. The "palace" was a large structure of bark and skins, with a sort of bedstead on one side, on which Powhatan sat with his robe of raccoon skins, and feathers in his hair.

When Smith and two of his companions were brought into the presence of this emperor, the scene was striking. Along each wall stood two rows of young women at the rear and two rows of men in front of them. The faces of all the women were stained red and a number wore chains of white beads around their necks. Smith doffed his hat, made a sweeping bow and addressed Powhatan with as much outward respect as if he had been the King of England.

Powhatan was angry and it was clear that he felt no good will toward those who dared to make their homes in his country. He pretended not to understand the broken sentences of his visitor until one of his warriors had helped to interpret them. Having met with no success, Smith and his friends withdrew and set sail down the river for Jamestown.

During the interview Smith and his companions had asked about the youth and the girl who had met them when first on their way up the James. But Nantaquas and Pocahontas were absent from the town—no other reason would have kept them from the palace on so interesting an occasion.

Smith wondered why an attack had not been made on the English long before. With the many warriors that Powhatan could summon, they would have been able to crush the little band of Europeans, despite the firearms at their command. Smith had no idea that the postponement of such an assault was due to Pocahontas—nor did he learn the truth until years afterward.

As his boat was making the moonlit journey back to Jamestown, a flickering movement along the northern shore caught his eye—it was an Indian canoe, in which he made out one person handling the paddle, with a companion sitting quietly in the stern. Smith watched it closely and was soon certain that the two persons were Nantaquas and Pocahontas. He had learned their identity from the friendly Indians who came to Jamestown: the plume worn by the girl was a badge of royalty. The canoe was passing the bow of the ship a hundred yards distant, making no attempt to come nearer. Wanting to talk, Smith called out:

"Nantaquas! Will you not come aboard?"

The youth seemed to exchange words with his sister, after which he headed his craft in the direction of the larger one. A few minutes would have brought him alongside, but he was brought up short by a startling interruption. Through the stillness a low, booming sound rolled upstream and echoed along the shore.

It was the sound of the cannon on the *Susan Constant*, many miles downstream. The blast alarmed Smith and his friends, for to them it could only have one meaning. It had been fired because of an attack by Indians on the settlement. Nantaquas instantly veered away, expecting a volley from the boat, but nothing of the kind occurred to Smith, who did not interfere while the canoe rapidly passed from sight.

Smith hurried to the stern, where the others had gathered. "The settlement has been attacked," he said. "Listen!"

Naturally, the certainty that there was trouble at Jamestown increased Smith's and his friends' impatience to reach the place as soon as they could. But the wind had stopped and the rising tide began to carry them back to Powhatan's capital. The anchor was dropped and the craft lay at rest, awaiting the turn of the tide or a rising of the wind.

The calm lasted through the night and when daylight came the tide had turned, but moved so slowly that Captain Smith told his skipper to let the anchor remain for a few hours. They ate the coarse bread they had brought and the fowl that Smith had shot on the upward voyage.

Smith's next words caused astonishment. He intended to go to the southern shore with two of his men to inquire into a signal fire he had seen the night before. He hoped to learn something of the trouble at Jamestown, and he hoped to find a way to obtain corn, which his countrymen needed. He knew that an Indian village was not far inland. There was reason to hope that through barter the owners could be persuaded to part with a good supply of food.

A number of trinkets and beads were bundled up and put in the boat. The three men took their places, with the Captain at the stern. When the boat touched land, they stepped out and awaited Smith's orders. Each man had a knife and a musket. Smith told his friends to go off by themselves.

The two men, Jack Bertram and Dan Wood, moved upstream. Wood walked in front, making the work easier for Bertram, who kept close behind. When they had pushed their way a short distance, Wood stopped.

"What good can come of this? No one has been this way. I don't understand what Captain Smith hopes to learn by this. Ah!"

Turning to resume their passage through the forest, Wood had caught sight of a well-marked trail leading over the course they were following. Wood walked for a few paces, scanning the path, which soon turned inland. Suddenly he halted. Glancing up, Bertram saw the reason.

Standing in the trail, staring at the two men, was the very girl they had seen when the ships were sailing up the James weeks before on their way to found the colony. She had the same rich robe around her shoulders and the same white plume curling over her long black hair.

She carried her long bow in one hand, the top of a quiver of arrows peeping from behind her left shoulder.

She caught sight of the white men before they saw her. She must have been coming over the path when she observed the figures and stopped in amazement.

"It is Pocahontas," whispered Bertram. "We did not see her yesterday at the old chief's lodge. I wonder what she can be doing here alone?"

"Her friends can't be far. I say, Jack, this is a godsend."

"What do you mean?"

"You'll see."

The girl did not hesitate once she realized that she had been observed by the strangers. She knew these men had come from Jamestown and she came smilingly forward. She had noticed the custom of the Englishmen of clasping their hands when they met. Without pausing, she reached out her hand to Wood, who was in front, and said to him in broken words:

"How do? How do? Me friend—you friend."

Wood took her hand, warmly pressed it, and then gave way to Bertram, who did the same. Pocahontas tried to say something more, but she knew so little English that neither caught her meaning. She saw that too many of her words were spoken in her own tongue, so, laughing, she gave up the effort and stood looking inquiringly into the faces before her.

"Jack," said Wood in a low voice, "the Indians have attacked Jamestown. We don't know how many of our people they have killed. We need food. Let's take this daughter of the old chief and hold her hostage. We'll give him the choice of letting us have all the corn we want—or of having his pet daughter put to death."

"I hardly know what to say to that. It might not work."

"It has to. Powhatan loves her so much that he will do anything to keep her from coming to harm."

Wood did not wait to argue further, but, taking a quick step toward the smiling girl, grasped her upper arm. In answer to her questioning look he said:

"Go with us. We take you to Jamestown. Won't hurt."

The smiles gave way to an expression of alarm. She held back.

"No, no, no! Me no go! Powhatan feel bad—much bad!"

"You must go!" said Wood, tightening his grip. "We not hurt you any."

Bertram stood silent—he didn't like the scheme, but he thought it might turn out well, so he didn't interfere.

And then Pocahontas began crying and striving to wrench her arm free. Had not Wood used all his strength, she would have gotten away. Impatient over her resistance, he tried to scare her into submission. Scowling at her, he said, in a brutal tone:

"Stop! Come with me or I will kill you!"

This was an idle threat. He thought nothing of the kind. But he probably would have struck her, for he was a quick-tempered man. Pocahontas struggled harder than ever, her moccasins sliding over the slippery leaves, tears streaming down her cheeks. She begged and prayed in her own language, not knowing the English words.

Meanwhile, Captain Smith had only gone a little way down the stream when he decided that he had taken the wrong course. He turned around and followed after his companions, coming upon them in the midst of the struggle between Wood and Powhatan's young daughter. He paused only an instant, when he angrily cried out:

"What is the meaning of this?"

Wood merely glanced around at his leader and kept on dragging the captive along the trail. It was Bertram who hastily said:

"She is the daughter of Powhatan. We are going to take her to Jamestown as a hostage and make the chieftain give us corn—"

Without waiting for anything further, the Captain sprang forward, shouting wrathfully:

"Let her go! Release her!"

Before the amazed fellow could comply, he was grasped by the back of the collar. Smith's fingers were like those of a giant, and the frightened Englishman let go of his sobbing prisoner. As he did so the Captain gave a kick with his right foot that lifted Wood clear of the ground, sending him tumbling on his face.

"I would do right to kill you!" cried Smith, his face aflame as he glared down on the fellow, who began climbing to his feet. "There is not one so good a friend of the English among all the Indians in Virginia as this little girl."

As he spoke he pointed toward the spot where Pocahontas had stood only a minute before, but she was not there. She had fled beyond sight.

Captain Smith's burst of anger was caused, in the first place, by the unpardonable violence shown to the young and gentle Pocahontas. In the sweetness of her nature she had shown perfect trust in the white men and everyone knew she had only friendship for the people who had made their homes in the country of her father, the great Powhatan. What a rude awakening for her! What harm would it bring to those who so badly needed the good will of the powerful tribes around them?

A second cause of the Captain's wrath was the fact that the outrage, apart from its wickedness, was the worst thing possible. If Wood had succeeded in taking Pocahontas hostage, Powhatan would not have been frightened into helping them; the act would have added to his ill will.

Not only that, but it was not to be supposed that Pocahontas was alone so far from home. She certainly had friends nearby—she would reach them soon and they would hasten to punish her enemies.

These thoughts flashed through the mind of Captain Smith, while the victim of his anger was slowly climbing to his feet. He took a step toward Wood, meaning to strike him to the earth again, but the man shrank away, with no word of protest. The Captain checked himself and said:

"We must hasten to the boat before we are cut off. Come!"

The fellow picked up his hat and gun, and Captain Smith led the way at a rapid pace till they reached the edge of the stream, along which they hurried to the spot where the craft had been left. Smith pushed it free and stepped in, followed by the other two, who sat down and caught up the oars.

The three had reached a point fifty yards from land when a young Indian warrior dashed through the undergrowth into the open space on the beach. He was Nantaquas—at his side was Pocahontas. He held his bow and drew an arrow from his quiver. The girl pointed excitedly to Wood, who was rowing and who was nearer to them than the others.

Captain Smith watched Nantaquas, not allowing any movement to escape him. Suddenly he called, "*Down!*"

Wood flung himself forward on his face, so that he was hidden by the side of the boat. Bertram dodged to one side. The Captain did not move. He knew *he* was in no danger.

Nantaquas' arrow streaked over the spot where the intended victim had been sitting. But for Wood's quickness, the arrow would have been buried in his chest. The oarsman regained his coolness. He raised his head and reached for his musket.

"Drop that!" thundered Captain Smith. "It would serve you right if you were killed! Use your oars!"

At any moment the Captain or his comrades could have shot Nantaquas, who stood in clear view, but the leader would not allow it. He sympathized with the Indian, and he would not permit any harm to be done to Nantaquas.

Nantaquas saw that if he fired again, the arrow was likely to hit Captain Smith. He knew which man had befriended Pocahontas, and eager

as he was to slay Wood, he would have to forgo that pleasure in order to spare the friend. Holding the long bow poised for a few seconds, he slowly lowered it. All this time the boat was moving rapidly and soon passed beyond bowshot.

Nantaquas remained standing on the shore, his sister beside him, both watching the craft until it came alongside the larger one. The three stepped aboard. Then brother and sister turned and passed into the forest.

A brisk breeze was blowing, and Captain Smith and his companions were carried at a good speed toward Jamestown, which they reached early that afternoon.

On the day that Captain Smith had sailed up the James River to make his call upon Powhatan, the colonists were engaged in cultivating the corn already put in the ground. Without warning, from the woods nearby came showers of arrows. Glimpses of the shouting Indians could be seen as they flitted from tree to tree. The panic-stricken English dropped their tools and ran behind the stockades. Those who glanced behind saw one man lying on his face, dead, pierced by many arrows. Nearly all the others had been hit, some of them two or three times— when they ran through the open gate the arrows were sticking in their bodies and clothing. The Englishmen could protect themselves, but could do little in the way of driving off their attackers, who were well shielded among the trees.

This is how things stood when the *Susan Constant*, came on the scene. Dropping a little way downstream, so as to get clear range of the woods, she fired two of her cannon. When the warriors saw tree limbs splintered and falling about their heads, they were terrified and scurried off in panic. Some time after dark, the settlers heard sounds in the woods that meant that their enemies had returned. The *Susan Constant*, then fired another shot, and this ended the trouble for some time to follow. It was the booming of this cannon that had traveled up the James to Smith's boat.

The first attack on Jamestown brought good results. It was clear to all that the settlement must have an industrious leader. Smith finally demanded his right to a trial to defend himself against the charges that were made long before—and for which he was still technically under arrest. Smith was given his trial, the first one by jury in America; and never did an accused man gain a greater triumph. Every charge brought against him was shown to be false, and one of his accusers had to pay him a fine!

Despite Smith's triumph, the miseries of that first summer in Jamestown were enormous. For a time it looked as if disease would claim the life of every man. If Powhatan had wanted to attack, he would have had no trouble in wiping out the colony. Even the sturdy Captain Smith took ill, but he didn't give up, and helped bury the dead.

By September, half the colonists had passed away, but the Indians were moved to pity and they brought corn to the sufferers, though only enough to last a short time. Sick and tired, the settlers now demanded that Smith take charge.

With the coming of the cool weather, disease subsided and those who had been ill rapidly recovered. The river abounded with fish and fowl, and corn was made into bread. The future looked bright. But now that the colonists believed they were out of danger, they criticized Smith because he had not begun to search for the South Sea—one of the reasons the King of England had sponsored the settlement. Smith declared that he would set out at once. It would be a relief to get away from the troubles and quarreling at Jamestown.

On a clear, cold day early in December, Smith started on his voyage in a barge with a crew of six Englishmen and two friendly Indians. He intended to go up the Chickahominy River, which empties into the James from a source far to the west.

The barge was provided with a sail, which could be helpful part of the time. It also had a small half-cabin at the stern in which the off-duty shift could sleep. There were three oarlocks on each side, to be used when the wind was not strong. Towed behind the barge was a smaller boat, which could be used when the river became too narrow for the barge. A supply of cornbread and venison was brought, but the party planned to rely on the fish and game they would catch.

It was still early in the day when the barge entered the mouth of the Chickahominy. Captain Smith sat at the stern, just behind the little cabin, his hand resting on the tiller. About the middle of the afternoon the breeze fell and the flapping sail told the navigators that they must use the oars.

Eventually, the large boat could go no further upstream. The small one in tow would now have to be used. Smith planned to go up the stream as far as he could in the smaller boat, but before leaving the barge, he sent his Indian scouts ashore to scour the woods for signs of the Indians whose hunting grounds they were now on.

Smith's scouts did not come back until late that night. They reported that they had not seen any of their own people in the vicinity. His men keeping watch on the boat did not notice anything, either. It seemed that no danger loomed.

The barge was then rowed to the middle of a wide stretch of water.

Smith decided to take the two Indians and two Englishmen with him. Wood and Bertram asked to go too, but their behavior toward Pocahontas might prove dangerous should they run into Powhatan's people.

"No matter what happens after I am gone," he told the four men who stayed on the barge, "not one of you is to go ashore. That might be just what the Indians are waiting for you to do."

So five men entered the boat, which had two pairs of oars but had no sail. Captain Smith had not been gone half an hour when those left behind in the barge started grumbling.

"It is unbearable to stay here for two or three days," said Wood, seated at the bow, looking glum. "How shall we spend the hours?"

"The scouts told us no Indians were near. Let's go ashore, where we can find game and stretch our limbs."

The proposal was against their leader's orders, but it appealed to all four men. Bertram and Wood rose to their feet and began plying their poles. They headed for a space favorable for stepping from the craft.

The side of the boat was so near the bank that it was a short jump for any of them. Wood stood still with his pole, ready to jump, when one of his friends shouted out:

"Back—quick! The woods are full of Indians!"

The four men on the boat did not lose their presence of mind. Wood and Bertram used the poles to the utmost, despite the arrows whizzing around them. They pushed so hard that the boat moved quickly and the space between it and the shore widened with every moment. Their companions aimed their muskets at the crowding forms along the bank, and fired with such skill that each brought down a warrior.

Bertram and Wood plied the poles, paying no attention to the missiles flying around them, while their companions reloaded and discharged the guns as quickly as possible. When the craft reached the middle of the broad space, little was to be feared from the Indians, for the distance was too great for them to aim well.

Wood had been hit, but was smiling over his good fortune at escaping, when he pitched forward on his face, pierced to the heart by one of the last arrows to be fired at the boat.

The body was tenderly laid in the stern, and then, while two men remained alert with their weapons, the third used the oars. There was no thought now of waiting for Captain Smith to come back. They did not believe he would return. So they kept on downstream as best they could. In due course they reached Jamestown and told their story. No one expected to see Captain John Smith and his companions again.

While the men on the barge were fighting for their lives, Smith and his party had traveled about a dozen miles before meeting their first barrier. Smith saw the little boat could go no further, so the men drew it up on the river bank.

"You are weary from rowing," he said to the oarsmen. "Wait here and rest while the two scouts and I go a little farther in search of game."

Smith meant to return before dark, when they could cook the game that he was sure of bagging, and they would spend the night in comfort by the campfire. Despite what the men said, they were quite worn out from rowing. So they kindled a fire and lay down with their feet to the flames. They sank into deep, restful sleep. Neither of them ever awoke again. Within an hour, the same party of Indians that had attacked the barge found them and ended their lives.

The leader of these Indians was called Opecancanough, one of Powhatan's brothers, and a very powerful warrior. Opecancanough never liked the English, and he urged Powhatan and his fellow warriors to destroy them. Opecancanough knew that Captain Smith was the most important man at Jamestown, and that killing him would be better than killing twenty other Englishmen. When he learned of the Chickahominy expedition, he gathered more than a hundred of his warriors and followed the boat for many miles, waiting for a chance to destroy the crew, especially Smith.

Now that Smith had left his boat, it was not hard for Opecancanough to trail him, since he could not go through the forest without leaving the prints of his shoes. As Smith tramped through the forest with the two friendly Indians, he began to think that what had threatened him along the way had passed, and that he need not worry anymore. He was peering among the branches of the trees and along the ground in search of game, and was growing impatient. Suddenly he saw a movement to the left that he knew was caused by some animal. Uttering a "Shh!," he stopped short and looked at the point where he had seen the movement.

The next moment he caught the outlines of a buck lurking among the trees. Afraid that the Indians might not have seen the stirring in the bushes, Smith turned his head to whisper a warning.

As he did so he saw only one of his men. The one who had been at the rear was gone. This discovery caused such a shudder of distrust that Smith forgot the buck and asked: "Where is he?"

The second scout flashed his head about, as astonished as Smith. He said: "He was behind me; I don't know what's become of him."

A crashing noise made them turn to the front. It was caused by the buck, which, having observed the hunter, was off like the wind. The Captain turned round again. The remaining scout was standing with his back to him, his long bow in his left hand, searching for his missing comrade. He seemed as puzzled as the Englishman.

Suddenly Smith saw another disturbance among the trees. An Indian appeared, coming cautiously toward him. Then another showed on the right, a third on his left, and beyond, around and among these, others were revealed, with still more coming into view. A band was approaching the startled Captain, who knew he was in trouble. The party that had slain three of his friends had caught up with him at last.

If there was any doubt as to their intentions, it was soon made clear when twenty of them sent their arrows flying among the trees and branches at the white man. Smith had his eye on the nearest Indian, who had come close to hitting him; noting that he was fitting a second arrow to his string, he aimed at the warrior and shot him dead.

Smith's scout was unable to move or speak. Although he held a fine bow, he made no attempt to use it. It was too much to expect him to attack his own people, when there was no chance of helping the white man by doing so.

Two steps brought the Captain so near to him that he could have touched his friend's back.

"Stand where you are! Don't move!" commanded Smith. "They won't shoot through you to reach me."

Smith managed to reload, keeping his body shielded by that of his Indian friend. The Captain saw that he should not fire until he had to. As Smith attempted to retreat, he saw that a warrior had worked so far to the right of him that he could no longer screen himself.

The warrior stepped from behind the trunk that had sheltered him and aimed at the slowly retreating Smith. Before he could fully draw the arrow, he cried out loudly and fell forward with his bow bent under him. Smith had fired again—and none too soon.

The unexpected shot stopped the warriors for a minute, giving Smith time to reload his weapon. He took a couple of steps back, saying to his scout, "We've got to keep moving until I tell you to stop."

At this point Smith noticed that one of the Indians had an English musket in his hands! Less than thirty feet away another warrior held a similar gun. Smith realized then that his two friends he had left in camp had been killed. He had nobody to fall back on.

Smith would have continued retreating and fighting until the warriors brought him down. He did not give up even when an arrow pierced his thigh. Then he noticed that the scout shielding him had also been hit. The Indians were growing impatient and were firing their arrows with less care for his safety; the scout's life would not be spared unless Smith moved aside.

Smith pushed his friend away. The Captain retreated faster, ready to use his musket the instant it was needed. He was moving so quickly he did not see where he placed his feet; he put his right foot down, but instead of finding firm support, the leg sank to the knee in soft mud. Smith made a desperate effort to wrench it free, but the left foot went down as far as the other. He struggled but sank farther, until both legs were imbedded in the ooze almost to his thighs. The clinging mud seemed colder than ice. He knew he would die, even if the Indians left him alone. He flung his musket away and threw up his hands.

"I yield! I surrender!" he cried in the Indians' language.

Most of the warriors feared to draw closer—Smith's gun had filled them with dread. The few with more courage went to the floundering man and grasped his outstretched hands, pulling him onto hard ground. His captors kindly rubbed the mud from his clothes and led him back to the camp where his dead friends lay.

Soon, a line of march was formed with Opecancanough in the center, the English swords and muskets carried as trophies before him. Next to him walked Smith, his arms held by two warriors.

The procession moved through the forest until it reached a hunting home of Powhatan, north of Chickahominy Swamp. This village had about forty houses. Women and children swarmed out and stared in amazement at the prisoner. The warriors began a grand war dance around Smith and Opecancanough. When they had finished they led Smith to a large matted wigwam, which he entered, while twenty Indians stood guard outside. Smith was unbound and he sat on a bearskin near the entrance to the lodge.

Several weeks followed in which Captain Smith was exhibited through the country, with crowds swarming to look at him like a circus animal. During this time Smith kept looking for Pocahontas or Nantaquas, hoping they would remember the kindness he had shown the girl. But he saw neither, since his travels were in Opecancanough's lands. Finally, Opecancanough brought the captive to Werowocomoco, before the mighty Powhatan himself. There the question of what to do with Smith would be settled.

The tall, haughty Powhatan sat on a framework suggestive of a throne, covered with mats, in front of a large fire. He was wrapped in a raccoon robe. On each side sat a young woman, two of his wives, and along the sides of the royal lodge stood two rows of men, with the same number of women standing behind them.

As Smith was brought before this imposing company, he knew that the Emperor was about to decide his fate, for the prisoner had been brought there to hear his sentence. As the Captain bowed to Powhatan he looked about for Pocahontas and Nantaquas, and saw the young warrior. He was standing on the right of the Emperor. His eyes met those of Smith. Whatever his feelings were, the youth gave no sign.

But where was Pocahontas? Twice Smith searched among the group, but that gentle face was not to be seen. The prisoner's heart sank.

Powhatan and his brother chiefs would have spared Smith, but for the fact that he had killed two of their people. That was an offense that could not be pardoned and so he was sentenced to death. Two warriors entered the lodge, each struggling to carry a heavy stone. The stones were placed together in front of the chieftain.

At a sign from Powhatan six of his men went over to Smith and pushed him forward, his hands tied behind his back; he was flung to the ground and his head forced down so that it rested on the stones.

Most of the warriors fell away, leaving one on either side of the captive. These stood near his shoulders and each held a huge club, in position for them to draw it back and bring it down on Smith's head with such force that no second blow would be needed.

All eyes were fixed upon Smith and his executioners. No sign of pity showed on the face of any of them. Powhatan did not give any command or speak, for it was not needed. The two with the clubs knew their duty.

In this tense moment, a movement was heard on the left of the Emperor. It was Pocahontas. With a gasping exclamation, she dashed between the men in front of her, thrusting them out of her way, and, bounding across the intervening space, dropped on one knee, placed an arm on either side of the Captain's head, and with tears streaming down her cheeks, looked up at her father.

"You must not kill him! He is my friend! He was kind to Pocahontas! Spare his life, dear father, for *me!*"

No one moved or spoke. Powhatan glared angrily at his daughter—neither she nor anyone else had ever dared to do a thing like this before. Had it been anyone else, he would have struck the person dead at his feet.

But he could not raise a hand against his beloved daughter. He started to rise, but changed his mind and sank back again. The executioners looked at him, awaiting his command and paying no attention to the girl kneeling between them, with her arms still around Captain Smith's neck. He looked up into her dark, pitying eyes and a warm tear fell on his bronzed forehead. With one hand Pocahontas brushed back the heavy brown hair that had dropped over his eyes, and smiling through her grief, said:

"You shall not be harmed! Your life is spared!"

"How can you know that, my good friend?"

"Don't you see?" she asked, trying to help him to his feet.

The warriors with their huge clubs had stepped away from the two. Powhatan could not deny the prayer of Pocahontas, and had signaled them to spare the life of the Englishman.

When Smith stood up, his face went red with embarrassment. Not knowing what to do, he stood staring at the ground. Pocahontas fluttered around him like a bird. She tried to untie the knots that bound his wrists behind his back, and though she would have succeeded in a few minutes, she was impatient. She beckoned to her brother, Nantaquas, who came quickly forward and cut the thongs with his knife. He turned inquiringly to Powhatan, who motioned for his son to take the man away. Taking the hand of the prisoner in his own, the youth led him out of the wigwam. Pocahontas did not follow, but did another thing that astonished the group. Forgetful of all his kingly dignity, Pocahontas bounded to the throne, flung her arms around her father's neck and sobbed with thankfulness, murmuring words only Powhatan could hear.

For the moment, the great chieftain forgot that he was King. He stroked his daughter's hair until she regained command of herself. He told her that he had spared the prisoner because he could deny nothing to her. Her face glowed, tears still shining, as she walked back to where she was before.

Meanwhile, Nantaquas took Smith to his own lodge at the eastern edge of the village. It was only a dozen feet in length and about eight feet wide, with a fire at one end, and animal skins and furs on the floor and walls.

"I shall always be grateful to you, Nantaquas."

"Your thanks belong to my sister," was the gentle reply.

"I know that, and she will dwell ever in my heart. Does this mean that my life is spared for a short time only?"

"I will learn. Wait till I come back."

The Indian youth slipped outside. Captain Smith sat down on one of the furs and thought over the strange things that had happened. He was still thinking when his friend returned.

Nantaquas had talked with Powhatan, who told him that Smith was to stay among the Indians, and give his time to making moccasins, bows and arrows, and especially beads, bells and copper trinkets for Pocahontas. The Captain accepted the proposal with great pleasure, for he knew that sooner or later he would return to Jamestown.

He took up the task with the same energy he put into everything, and pleased Nantaquas, who showed a real friendship for him. Powhatan

was also quite satisfied, and Pocahontas, who often came to the little workshop and watched the sturdy captain at work, was delighted. She would sometimes sit for hours at a time on a mat in front of him, noting with great interest the movements of the skillful fingers that worked so deftly, though they were more used to handling a sword than to making delicate ornaments and trinkets. She could not restrain her happiness as the articles gradually took form.

When the Captain finished a pair of moccasins that were as dainty as Cinderella's slippers, Pocahontas slipped them on her feet, clapped her hands and danced about the wigwam. Nantaquas and Captain Smith smiled at the pretty picture, and the brave and good Captain felt well rewarded for his efforts. Indeed, could he ever repay this sweet daughter of the forest for what she had done for him? He often asked himself the question, and the answer was always a soft, but heartfelt, "No!"

Powhatan left no doubt of his friendly feelings toward Captain Smith, when, six weeks after he had started on his voyage up the Chickahominy, the chieftain allowed him to return under guard to Jamestown. He received a warm welcome from his countrymen.

Hard times now came to Jamestown. The people began starving to death. The famished settlers staggered along the street, too feeble to rise when they stumbled and fell. It looked as if no one would be left alive; the only one who kept on his feet was Captain Smith, who helped others with his unfailing good spirits.

But the day came when even Smith began to give up hope. Standing gloomily outside the palisades, looking off to the forest, he suddenly saw a strange sight. A girl came out from among the trees, bearing a basket of corn on her shoulder. He had hardly time to recognize her as Pocahontas, when he saw she was followed by eighteen other Indians, each carrying a basket of corn and other food. Next to her was Nantaquas. If not for this kindness, all the settlers would have died.

The grateful Englishmen referred to this good maiden ever after as "the dear and blessed Pocahontas." She came once or twice a week for months, bringing supplies through the woods to Jamestown. She had convinced Powhatan that it would be best for everyone if the Indians helped the white men. And even though there was often fighting between the two peoples, Pocahontas never weakened in her friendship to the colonists.

Sometimes Pocahontas' father became angry with her, and though parent and child did not quarrel, the girl only became more guarded in her deeds of kindness, especially when Powhatan was at war with the Englishmen.

During one of these wars, Smith set out one day with a company to surprise Powhatan. He had not been gone long when nine of those he had left at home went out in a boat in a severe storm. The boat turned over and everyone in it drowned. Since Smith was counting on these men as backups, it was important that he be told of the accident.

The task of reaching Smith through miles of wilderness was so dangerous that only one man in the colony was willing to go. He was soon captured by the Indians and taken before Powhatan, who ordered him to be put to death. Without drawing suspicion to herself, Pocahontas was able to get the white man a short distance away, and then hid him among the bushes. He would have been found and brought back by the warriors who were searching for him had she not led them in the wrong direction. The man gained enough of a start to join Smith and tell him what had happened to the men he had counted on for help.

Some time later, when matters seemed to have quieted down, a party of colonists went among Powhatan's people to trade, but all except one man were massacred. Pocahontas succeeded in saving his life, and he lived among the Indians for many years, secure in her friendship.

Three years after Captain Smith and his fellow settlers had arrived in the land of Powhatan, Smith returned to England. He never came back, and after his departure, the settlement suffered even greater losses. When Smith left, there were five hundred men in Jamestown; only sixty were alive at the end of six months. Gradually, though, conditions improved and more and more people came from England to settle in the

colony. Many of these people tried to take advantage of the Indians, and even Pocahontas, who had always acted on behalf of the colonists, was not safe when there was fighting between her people and the English.

One of the English captains, Samuel Argall, was an explorer and adventurer like Captain Smith. Early in 1613, while leading an expedition up the Potomac River to find corn for the settlers, he met Pocahontas and another Indian woman who sometimes accompanied her on her walks. Pocahontas, though she was a young woman now, still looked much the same as when Smith first saw her in the canoe with Nantaquas. She still held a great affection for the English and did not hesitate when Captain Argall invited her to visit his ship. Suspecting no evil, Pocahontas came aboard with her companion. Unknown to the Indian Princess, however, the woman had been bribed with Argall's promise that no harm would come to Pocahontas. When the woman went back ashore, Pocahontas was kept prisoner. Argall's expectation was that Powhatan would be glad to pay a huge ransom in corn for her return to him. But instead of doing so, the furious chieftain prepared to wage an even fiercer war against the colony.

During these troubling weeks Pocahontas stayed at Jamestown, where everyone treated her kindly. At this time, Pocahontas learned more about the English people's way of life and their religion. Taking their beliefs to heart, she converted to Christianity and was baptized and given a new name, Rebecca.

John Rolfe, a member of a good English family, fell in love with Pocahontas, and she returned his affection. The two were married in April 1613. Although Powhatan did not attend the ceremony, he cheerfully gave his consent and sent his brother and two of his sons to represent him. One of them was Nantaquas, who was very pleased with the marriage. Pocahontas' uncle gave her away in accordance with Anglican ritual. The windows were decorated with evergreens, wild flowers and crimson holly berries. The settlers and Indians crowded the small building, gazing upon the beautiful scene. The marriage was happy in all ways. Husband and wife loved each other, and Powhatan became the true friend of the English, and remained so to the end of his life.

When the English Governor, Sir Thomas Dale, sailed for England in 1616, he took Rolfe and Pocahontas, or "Lady Rebecca," with him. She received a great deal of attention from the royal court and was well loved by the people she met. Everyone was eager to make her happy in this new and strange land.

Pocahontas was anxious to meet her old friend, John Smith. He was the first person she asked about. But, to her grief, she was told that he was dead. While she was in mourning for him, Captain Smith came to see her. She was so shocked that she burst into tears.

She soon regained her cheerfulness and the two sat down and had a long talk over their lives in America, three thousand miles away. She called the Captain "father," and he returned the honor by calling her "daughter."

In 1617, Rolfe and his wife made ready to return to the New World, when Pocahontas fell ill and died at the age of twenty-one. Her infant son, Thomas, was taken to London and educated by his uncle, Henry Rolfe. But when he reached adulthood, he sailed to America, back to the land that was his mother's home.